The Poetic Vibrations of a Matured Butterfly

Arthur Lee Conway

© 2021 Arthur Lee Conway. All Rights Reserved.

No part of this book may be reproduced, stored in a retrieval system, or transmitted by any means without the written permission of the author.

ISBN: 978-0-578-25193-6 (e)
ISBN: 978-0-578-95346-5 (sc)

Reprint
Printed in the United States of America

Illustrated by Hampton R. Olfus, Jr.

Dedicated

to my personal butterfly
Ollie Ervis Harris Conway

TABLE OF CONTENTS

RITES OF PASSAGE..1

VALLEY OF PASSIONS..31

PHILOSOPHICAL ROADS..75

Rites of Passage

The Consequences of a Blackman Bringing Fire

A Blackman was found lying on a Memphis hotel's balcony, his brains shattered like sand bursting in air, after being tossed from a child's little hand. Some say he looked like Buddha resting in a grove of sandalwood trees; others claimed that he favored Jesus Christ on Mt. Cavalry, or was it, Lao Tse....

Yet, many people claimed they had never seen nor heard of those mystifying Civilers of centerness before.

Nevertheless, some people said," The Blackman looked like Prometheus, who was bound to the mountainside for stealing Fire and, sharing it with Mankind". And, as Irony would have it, the Vultures of the New World Order plucked at his liver viciously, feeding like a pack of wolves upon a warm lamb's carcass.

But, the Vulgus never noticed the ravishment of the Blackman, as they continued to travel back and forth... up and down the mountain with torches of Fire; that would flicker out as if they had been doused with water; as the self-appointed Carriers of Fire got closer to the earth's surface. The Carriers were like Sisyphus, the Stone-pusher of perpetual retrogression.

Though it did not seem to matter, as the Infinite Absolute released another cosmic ray of Divine Light that would impregnate the ever fertile Womb of Maya... causing once again; a faint stirring in the cocoons of the Butterfly People.

Untitled #4

A wingless citified Man child lies cracked opened
split from head to toe by a fusillade of lead,
as a childish fist squeezes a gram of rock tightly,
as his brains seep out like rain, flowing down a ghetto sewer, quickly
mixing with Urbania's decay. As a pair of eyes look coldly yet passionately
at Eziekel's wheel spinning like a dervish in God's
heaven… as a woman screams & screams and moans
from a second floor window; pulling viciously at her uncombed hair like
an epileptic biting determinedly upon a spoon, as school children gather
around like ants meandering over a morsel of fungus-filled bread; little
fingers point lethargically like elephants sluggishly wagging their massive
tails at nagging flies, as a body rests quietly in Street's soulless arms.

After The Wedding

Woman in wheelchair
…pageantry of people whirling
by her like a merry-go-round.

Currency

I dreamt of God:

He was green

With silver finger nails

And teeth

Of gold. And human!

The Gambler That Loved

LIKE A SIAMESE CAT RUBBING, ENCIRCLING A MAN'S LONE LEG WITH ITS FURRY BODY; LADY CHANCE PRESSED HER LUSCIOUS, FULL BOSOM AGAINST THE GAMBLER'S HEAD: A NIPPLE LIGHTLY GRAZED THE BASE OF HIS NECK; SENDING A RUSH DOWN HIS BACK, AS HE SAT AT THE KITCHEN TABLE. SHE TEASED HIS THOUGHTS LIKE A MASSEUSE SQUEEZING AND PULLING MALLEABLE FLESH: DISSIPATING STRESS. HE SMILED WHILE THUMBING THROUGH HIS TICKETS LIKE A FOX IN THE HOT PURSUIT OF A RABBIT SEARCHING FOR THE ONE HE THOUGHT HE PLAYED. SUDDENLY, LIKE A VICTORIAN SCHOOLMASTER BERATING A STUDENT FOR SOME ASSUMED IMPROPRIETY, THE GAMBLER STARTED CURSING LADY CHANCE FOR TOUCHING HIM IN SUCH AN OBSCENE WAY…

"BITCH, WILL YOU PLEASE LEAVE ME ALONE!" HE CURSED, AS HIS RIGHT HAND SWEPT ACROSS THE TABLE, PUSHING VIGOROUSLY THE TICKETS ONTO THE KITCHEN FLOOR.

Urban Graphics I

Twisted shivering bodies dressing doorways
like near-dead Jews filling Buchenwald
graves… begging alms.

An Abrupt Flash of Hell in Urbania

White jackets flapping and billowing like kites in a March wind.
A litter being pushed like a bobsled in an Olympian race.
A glittering blade slicing flesh like a butcher trimming fat…
A spool of thread standing by like a Buckingham
Palace guard awaiting a command.
A geyser of red rushing upward like Mt. Helen
violently spewing molten ash into the heavens.
A pair of hands moving feverishly like a Japanese sumo wrestler struggling
with his opponent, trying to seize Victory.
An oscilloscope bleeping like a naval vessel's sonar searching Poseidon's
dark abode… for the enemy's presence.
A lead ball lost in fleshy fields: located.
As a group of weary men and women yell, "All Right!"

Culprit?

OPPRESSION is
being forced upon the Welfare rolls
& accepting, because one's instincts
require one to survive by any means necessary.

The Life and Times of a Man

Morning sunlight stealing its half of a house
reeking with Melancholy's odoriferous scent... as
a key massage cold, lifeless, metal tumblers,
arousing them... forcing a door's
orifice open, as a couch sighs quietly, passionately engulfing an old lost
Warrior that routinely now,
enter its soft folds...
while bedsprings squeak & moan above his head.

The Hunt

Once upon a time in the City of Angels, a Kafkaesque character named R.K. was motoring along at a top rate of speed... zipping through the urban jungle of Sinclairian madness. When like a sudden nuclear flash, a group of soldiers in a squad car with the LAPD emblem on the door appeared; they were pointing, signaling with their stubby fingers for him to pull over. R.K. was not certain of their intentions; seeing that it was quite dark outside, he just sped away. That impulsive act only spurred, fueled the soldiers seething desire for the kill. R.K. held the pedal against the metal as the car shot through the city street like a jackrabbit racing ahead of a coyote. But to no avail, because like a pack of wolves chasing their prey... they got stronger as the aromatic smell of blood filled their nostrils. R.K. slowed. Finally, R.K. and his friends were surrounded like a bunch of pioneers cowering (see R.K. was not alone) in their covered wagons, while hostile Indians circle them like one might see in a good old John Wayne B movie.

"Get out of the car, Mr. Fox!" yelled the soldier in charge.

R.K. appeared like some mysterious Kafkaian insect as he struggled to extricate himself from the driver's seat.... Suddenly, It started wriggling its spiny legs or was it his arms. The soldiers jumped back as if they had encountered a little child with a hand grenade in its hand, about ready to pull the pin.

"What the hell is it?" a face screamed from the back of the pack.

Instantly, the soldiers regained their fragile composure and rushed forward with nightsticks raised like a phalanx of Roman soldiers with spears in their hands. The air was charged with electrical violences as if a thunderstorm had erupted. As the men began beating, pounding, and smashing R.K.'s head: his back, legs, every available space on his body. He emitted a shrill cry like an insect in distress, but nobody heard his death cry. One could only hear what seemed like the
baying of the men; yes, they were like hounds upon the prey.

"Hold It down, hold It down… put your foot on It… stomp the m.f. Damn, it's strong! Almost like trying to subdue a panther!" bellowed one soldier while kicking the Object on the ground.

"Smash its fucking shell… I hate pest!" one soldier shrieked as he started crying like a baby.

As another soldier/policeman with somewhat of an angelic face became hysterical, gesturing with his finger… pointing relentlessly at The Object… The It that laid withering on the ground.

"It's bleeding…! It's a Man, I think…," the policeman's voice becoming almost inaudible. As the policemen just stared into the still womb of Night.

OPPRESSION is
discovering that your
daughter is hooked on crack…
& pregnant.

The Defilement of a Boarder Baby

I

a Boarder baby staring into Nothingness,
eyes bulging like a frightened frog being
seized by a lurking snake.

II

a Boarder baby screaming like a Banshee…
as she's impaled upon a crack crazed
phallus; that pushes like a stiletto
into her chaste womb, ripping flesh
like a red hot poker, neurons disarranged;
yelling like a heretic being roasted
at the gates of Seville, as a cryptogenic
man's anatomy jerks… a spray of semen leaps
forward like beads of sweat slung from the taut muscles
of a galloping racehorse… odorous sperm that smells of Mephistopheles'
bowels… commingling with an angel's
flowing blood.

…a Boarder baby screams, knowing not why.

When an Eagle Clips its Own Wings

for a classmate

...away he went like a tumbleweed dancing
in the wind, with the family's jewels in his soul. Creeping like
a ballet dancer on bent toes, trying to remain silent:
face Grief in solitude.
As an old rickety screen door squeaks on its hinges like a cemetery's
un-used iron gate. A voice reverberating through hollow halls like a spirit
being channeled through a psychic guide:
a feminine call of hope. But to no avail!
For he was determined to steal his loved one's
gold, stash it by the railroad tracks....
O, what a sly soul! As the house suddenly woke up to the squeals of steel
wheels that sounded like a million cicadas shouting... as the conductor begged for
Divine intervention; though all efforts amounted to nothing-as a massive engine
slammed against a helpless
frame like a lion severing an antelope's main vein..., as a
little boy dreams of an eagle with clipped wings.

OPPRESSION is
watching Kitty Genovese
being stabbed to death,
as her assailant scampers away
into Night's dark womb, when suddenly
one realizes that tomorrow
is another workday. As a woman's screams ring
like, Notre Dame's cathedral bells in one's head.

The Acrobat

Like a gymnastic silkworm
somersaulting on its thin threads,
an amputee performs graceful acrobatic
moves; circus stunts on his iron chariot
of life like an ambidextrous beast swinging
on bars, caged bars…,
as an evening bunch of merry onlookers stare
like Brueghel's figures of naive reasoning.

Rhapsody of an A-10 Thunderbolt

Myrtle Beach Air Force Base, SC

a black titanium belly
      glistening in the damp morning mist
           …birds chirping betwixt a knifing hum.

OPPRESSION is
being a full-fledged American
& waking up in a rock-strewn Internment Camp
for having slanted eyes... & dancing with **Calvin**
and **The American Enterprise Band.**

The Altered State of a Robin, or a Lightning Sketch of Western Civilization While Watching an American Queen Moonwalking

Like a Robin swaying limply as Pesticide's bacchanalian-like spirits sink into its little soul... an ancient African queen bobs & weaves with her musical Goebbelian ears stuck inside of Holy ears, hypnotized by an electronic Shellian monster propagating Hitler's BOOGIE-ON-DOWN-FOXTROT... for incapacitated minds, as Wagner's Nordic Valkyrie emits fiery screams of operatic madness; sounds of bleating chords of animalistic superiority, Nietzschean clowns dragging/leading frigid men & women into satanic acts of twirling, midnight dancing around Baroque hallways, as tears stream down Reality's face... as Black Kettle's bloody scalp leap and beat, beat Hard Backside Custer's de Sadian-like thighs, as Mengele extracts gold, gold & more gold from open mouths of incarcerated Jews, while Torquemada decimates Spain's Middle Class for Church & State... may we rest in God's grace, as Gypsies watch their hair being removed like lamb wool... taken away

like Tall Bull's flowing locks that stimulate, nauseate, mesmerizes savage thoughts, comatose egotism... devilistic bio-rhythms in institutionalized Zombies. Still, Goebbel's ghost continues pumping, pumping blues songs... iron blues, as W.B. Reynolds' antiquated mask is stored away in antebellum closets... for future acts of terror, & Charles 'Burger' Hughes' Court chalked up another victory for MEGA-BUSINESS... as The Nuremberg Tribunal of 1935; rescind all Jewish Rights, quickly

...**Affirmative Action & Other Affiliates** commence to take immediate action, curling like armadillos, trapping themselves in their own armored shells. While Lady Justice starts shivering & sweating like a Junkie cold turkeying... she yells, balls herself in the fetus mode, crying that she needs a Rooseveltian fix... as Men in long dark parliamentarian-like robes kick & flay her with steel rhetoric:

"KNEEL DOWN WOMAN, FOR WE ARE MEN...APPOINTED BY GOD TO DICTATE", they bellow, as perspiration gathers on their brows like patrons of a private burlesque show, while THE MASSES look quietly through a prism of mental confusion... HEY, DID ANYONE HEAR ABOUT THAT LIFE-THREATENING ASSAULT? Did you see Kitty Genovese's assailant? a handful of near speechless LEGAL CLONES inquired, at least claimed, that it gave them a case of NATURAL BLUES; that diarrheic kind, just like an old fashion Brownsvilles lynching... as a CROWD of 20th CENTURY FOX NAACPERS clap their hands like a group of Frankensteins standing around a bonfire. While a Nation of dark Pallbearers walks somberly with A. Philip Randolph's bones held high... as passing thoughts of his prowess float through their Mind's eye... as a congregation of ashen-faced people scream out like Cicero addressing a Roman senate:

"JUSTICE FOR MOVE! LONG SHALL WE REMEMBER THE PHILADELPHIA HOLOCAUST"

Ah, remember Tulsa,
Guernica,
Armenia,
Nagasaki,
Bikini Atoll?,

an imitation RABBLE ROUSER asked, while Ellison watched with tears in his eyes, as Dubois tossed & turned in his grave & Ghana cried for her restless son who could not enjoy his soulful slumber, for he never forgot that awesome face of a nightmarish beast called Racism; even as he lay in Death's loving arms. And like Turkish women lamenting their departed loved ones, Mother Africa wailed fiercely for her confused CHILDREN that remained in Diaspora's deadly claws of mechanical bondage, but wait, wait, I hear something... someone talking about WORKERS... Gompers, is that you Gompers? But, Gompers, I thought you were dead like JIM APARTHEID CROW...?, as a former African queen rocks & sways, swaying with a mind full of **ECSTASY** & steel rhythms, dead beats, dead beats, as a Nation becomes fascinated with The 360 Degrees New American Swing, just like George Valois' Le Faisceau dancers that loved waltzing with that maiden called Insanity... as an Astro-Cowboy come roaring & belching through heavenly skies like a Cessna with engine troubles; pulling a Don Quixote-like imitation of a lady called Manifest Destiny... a
skeletal looking female that desperately, mysteriously attempts... cuddles closely placards near her

milkless breast; cardboards with faces of deceased men:

        Jackson, Taft, Teddy,
        Wilson, Calvin, Hoover, McCarthy...
        NERO WITH A TORCH!

The Avenue, or the Day Marcia Williams was Killed

a stray bullet smashing a window
like a fallen chandelier shattering
against a marble floor: a spray of hair
sweeping across an un-attended steering wheel
like a peacock's feathers… children staggering
out of now unfamiliar doors; racing
into the mist of terror-stricken faces flanking an ever restive Avenue.

A Moment in the Life of Little Heart-bewildered

Camp Goodwill, Dumfries, VA

I

Little Heart-Bewildered romping
around his wooded playground,
like a hummingbirds fluttering dance
over a peach blossom.

II

Little Heart-Bewildered slipping
into a country stream like a Monarch
unknowingly, lighting upon a Wolf spider's web.

Wisdom and Age...

Wisdom and Age
got skipped over
by Sons and Daughters
that thought they were dead.

Expressed Manhood

Expressed manhood
without any base of intelligence,
is like an apple tree that produces no apples.

Valley of Passions

…A MOMENT OF MISDIRECTED IMPULSIVENESS

…a moment of misdirected impulsiveness
on the part of the instinctive dragonfly, can
mean that death might just arrive as swiftly
as his untimely actions; turning him into food
for the fish of the sea.

THE CHIMERICAL MOMENTS OF A MILWAUKEEAN CANDYMAN

...while standing in the confines of that famed Milwaukeean Police Dept., camera lights flashed from all angles like a premiere of some Stephen King movie, capturing a parade of celebrities on strips of celluloid, as Jeffrey 'The Candy Man' Dahmer requested a Hershey Milk chocolate bar. One officer leaped like a jack-in-the-box to accommodate him; jerking on a silver knob of a seemingly smiling vending machine, as a piece of candy wrapped in glossy brown paper hit down with a thud, like a body in a state of rigor mortis being dropped on a hot tin roof... as a Pavlovian shiver rocketed through his statuesque physique like a falling star; triggering him to reach out and grab it (by the way, Wisconsin state law forbids using bonds for a child molester),

...he quickly unwrapped that precious bar; stuffing it into a salivating mouth, chewing upon it vigorously, momentarily pausing like a squirrel with an acorn; just long enough to vent his distaste for homosexuals and Blacks... as Candy Man's un-cuffed right hand beat nervously against his thigh with a copy of Oscar Wilde's Dorian Gray (a young dark-complexioned youth with glasses, looking like Spike Lee had shoved the book defiantly into his left hand. Making that lone handcuff around his wrist jump like a disturbed rope.)

As a reporter pushed a microphone in Dahmer's direction, needling the Candy Man about his thoughts concerning "The Frances Cress Welsing Theory." But he only looked straight ahead like a good Prussian soldier awaiting Bismarck's review... lightly bantering about being a medic in the WAR, after spotting in the hungry crowd a man dressed in a white uniform... suddenly, he became distant like a migratory bird in flight, quite distant, as if his mental lights had been flicked off by some mysterious dybbuk. Nonchalantly, he just kept munching on a melting Hershey Milk chocolate bar, and like an incognizant neurotic, Dahmer thumbed each page of Wilde's book.

So much for Oscar and The Crest Theory.

THE GAME OF DECEIT IS LIKE PLAYING RUSSIAN ROULETTE

The game of Deceit is like playing Russian Roulette,
and it's never clear in a man's mind when he might
just chamber a round of trickery that may bring about his own demise.

OPPRESSION is
a little British child
in Middlesex...
spending her formative years
as a nuclear deterrent.

A PROGRESSIVE ACT OF LAND REFORM, AS VIEWED BY A LATIN AMERICAN CHILD

El Salvador, November 1989

Cold black-eyed Child staring
out of a cracked windowpane…
brown earth-flesh exploding;
splattering against a tin Casa
like rain falling upon an empty Campbell's
soup can.

INSTITUTIONALIZATION OF FAITH I

Some Churches conduct their spiritual affairs
like the many New York brokerages houses, where
a Worshiper can make an investment in the stocks
of the Spoken Word and receive dividends by way
of instilled faith.

STONED LIVING

There was a Lady that loved collecting rocks, she found that hoarding rocks provided her with a peculiar inner peace. One day after returning home from the doldrums of her workplace; she flopped down on her sofa, only to be frightened by some strange looking Lizard crying for help. It stared ever so often into her lined face.
It looked like a chameleon. Startled by such a ghastly creature, she instinctively grabbed one of her prized Rocks from the coffee table, striking it squarely on the head. The Lizard slumped backwards; it began to tremble, as if its autonomic nervous system had come to rule its helpless body. The Lady only gazed mindlessly at the bleeding Lizard, which slowly changed into something that she once loved watching.

OPPRESSION is
a throng of religious Fanatics
feuding and wrestling over a monotheistic
Deity of Chaos and Peace.

A SURREALISTIC SUPPER IN SOUTH AFRICA

...a lithe Bantu woman with steely black eyes sits
by a window in Soweto, mechanically, stubbornly she twists a gourd,
grinding diligently grey matter in a tin bowl....
Biko's brain?

Quietly, she grips the windowsill, pulling herself up from a wooden stool, and enters her smallish kitchen. She stands over the stove and watches leaping flames; staring blankly into a cloud of steam that sweeps upward towards heaven like African spirits of old... she starts sprinkling her food lightly with a mystical concoction while watching it rise like yeast filled bread, as an array of soul-fired young folks wait outside.

OPPRESSION is
looking at the weary
eyes & bloated bellies of children
surviving in Eritrea & other locales
of Arian festivities.

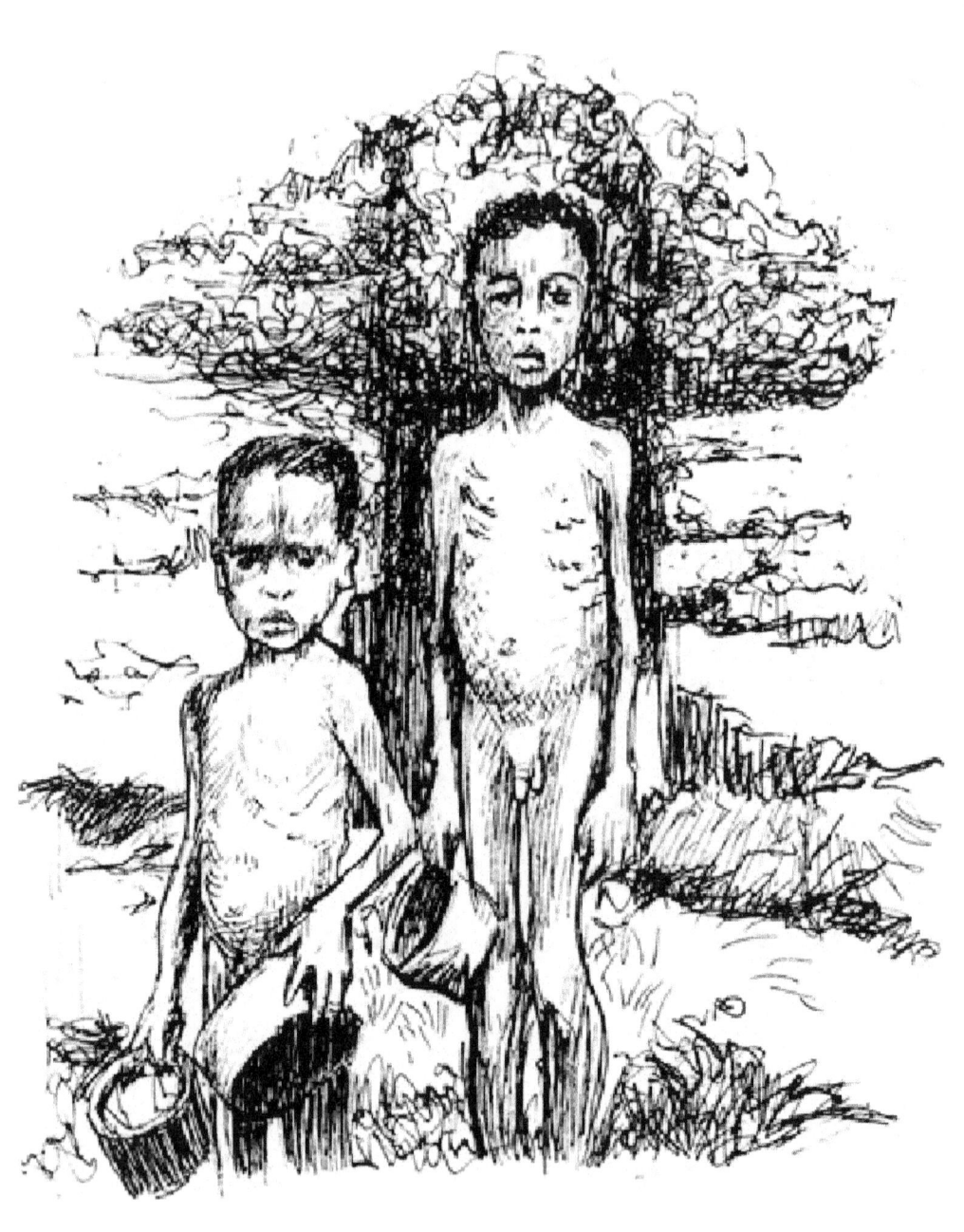

POLITICAL NURSING IN THE 21st CENTURY, AS EXPERIENCED BY A DEVELOPING LATIN AMERICAN CHILD

A little Latino baby
nursing on an American bovine's tit,
   gnashing its formative teeth
      against the beast's breast
         ...drawing blood.

PILLAGE II

The economic pillage of a Nation
is like Agamemnon forcibly taking Briseis
from Achilles

…demoralizing.

OPPRESSION is
a thousand Algerians being
tossed into the Valley of Death,
by maniacal Frenchmen that wish
to deny them that paradoxical touch
of European Enlightenment.

THE PERSONA OF STATESMANSHIP

In the U.S.
John Foster Dulles was
Viewed as a Statesman
of <u>High Integrity</u>
Like Ribbentrop assuaged himself:
With his diplomatic espousing of <u>Peace through Strength</u>
& <u>Lebensraum</u>...
While toting a weighted Hitlerian suitcase of new-found Aryanism.

SUBMERGED IN THE VALLEY OF COITUS

Black Love moving sensuously underneath me,
as I slide like water down a fall, over... across
my sweet BIk Love's finely sculptured ebony body;
coming together as Rather wrestles with Coltrane's
Africa... sizzling sounds that galvanize our passionate souls. As Dan's
voice echoes like thunder, supersonic **BOOMS** rush out of boobtube's
glassy face, as he speaks continuously of bombs raining down upon
Gibran's ancient homeland... falling... falling down on Verdun,
Tulsa, Ethiopia, Guernica, Manchuria, Poland's Warsaw Ghettoes,
Dresden, Covington, Hiroshima, Hanoi... Dominican Republic, Laos,
Afghanistan, Grenada, 61st & Osage, etc., etc...., bombs shitting shrapnel
every fucking where, as maimed holy-minded children look bewildered,
listlessly at bandages that clumsily mask stubby joints, as broken olive
branches poke their shattered limbs meekly through blood-soaked soil;
choking themselves to death in the sulfurous-filled air, while Blk Love and
I come...
come, cry out together, locking out Ariels' nameless icons of
destruction... that whine...scream; slice through Beirut's guts like un-
guided laser beams burning flesh needlessly. Still, Blk Love and I will fully
close our mind-doors on Pandora's Heydrich-like lunacy, as everything
becomes seemingly quiet like a child's peaceful hissing, faint hypnotic
sounds that float through a room filled with Summer's evening breath.

WAKING GIBRAN'S SPIRIT....

February 9,1984

Gibran's spirit screamed
Like a dervish whirling
Through his mystical ritual
Of infinite peace with Self...
like An Ashanti warrior being branded
With a smoldering slaver's iron... like Jesus
Reaching for God's rejuvenating touch...,

As that famed Lady of World War II vintage:
USS New Jersey
Whipped Lebanon into political submission;
With explosive
Shells of Hell... as Gamayel looked on
Like King Farouk
Watched England has its sexual-fill of Egypt.

UNTITLED #7

Grenada, 1983

I stood as one with my King, so unconcerned...
unaware of your presence... your heat of despair
with self,
(were you bothered by my uppity nature,
upset because I loved my Man...,
refused to notice you on the World stage?

Is that wrong'?

Yes, I guess that was your problem!
Because like all men... all Conquerors...,
you came... came like Cortes entered Montezuma'
house... guns & mental-shields; locked arm in arm
with Greed & Death, casting him
into a personal Nightmare!

...& now Bishop's home.
Why?

OPPRESSION is
being forcefully
taken away from one's
home at three o'clock
in the morning by a bunch
of rowdy Skinheads...
for a trip to Camp Unknown.

OPPRESSION is
watching the madmen
of Nuremberg being sentenced
to die on the gallows, while all
those Men that laid waste to Dresden,
Hiroshima, Manchuria & other human-filled
localities of the peasantry, go un-encumbered;
back into their mental Sacher-Masoch/Sadian
dormitories to bathe forever in un-claimed guilt.

A BEIJING STUDENT DREAMING....

I dreamt of a Red Dragon emerging
from a White Dragon with a sword
& shield in its webbed claws.
Suddenly, I turned to seek the aid
of the White Dragon, but he was nowhere
around; I only found a bunch of skeletal
bones... in the shape of a dragon. A dragon?

ORWELLIAN YEARS I

In the Orwellian years...
People were like ancient Birds
Lightning through earthly, concrete
Skies of disinformation. Yes, mentally,
They were like Kiwis in physique...
vestiges of evolution.

ORWELLIAN YEARS II

In the Orwellian years...
Sobriety testing became
Like honey in the minds
Of moralistic individuals,
That elected to savor only
Its disguised sweetness of legalism.
Yet, never noticing all those Franco-Hitlerian
Like stingers from days of old, that floated
Around in a paramilitary jar of justice.

ORWELLIAN YEAR III

In the Orwellian years...
Every sane offer of international
Diplomacy looked like a Trojan Horse,
Trying quietly to squeeze himself
Through busy Frankfurt Airport's
Rushing crowd.

ORWELLIAN YEARS IV

In the Orwellian years…
Blind Patriotism was called
Freedom, while Collectivism
Remained entangled within a political
Web of phraseology & linguistics.

DICTATOR III

Dictators are victims of constant paranoia…,
never knowing when a truncheon of foreign Discontent might smash their cranium.

GREEK MASKS OF COMEDY

Greek masks of comedy, quickly
    Strolling across Life's transparent
        Mirror of quiet tragedy.

DISCOTHEQUE AMELIA EARHART, OR THE CIRCLE

...DAZZLING LIGHTS ENERGIZING A CIRCUS OF PEOPLE... supernovas exploding: spraying a spectrum of multi-colored beams, drowning August Dog days in a flood of flashing musical stars. As frauleins cry like Senegalese women lamenting their men's departure for France's feast of vultures... as Freudian thoughts burst through fences of apollonian love... promises made in Reality's shade. While Hendrix's "Purple Haze" plays: cosmic rays explode like Vietnamese children skin peeling, crackling... disintegrating under Napalm's fiery breath, as heavenly white dwarfs pulsate faintly... spewing forth hallucinogenic worlds, as distant constellations appear on Carrollian walls of grey matter. As warriors grind against girlish thighs...
like back home before Uncle Sam's call
in sweaty rural roadside clubs of bigotry, like in dimly lit ghetto basements humming love songs; as soldiers yelp & howl at tonic-filled lyrics of soulful men singing "Stay in my Corner" & Freida Payne crying
"Send the Boys Home," as crotches discharge Dionysian-like moisture of fuck. While cannon fodders burn mental pictures of their women in Amerika...BURN THEM UP LIKE HIPPIES SETTING AFLAME DRAFT CARDS IN BOSTON SUBURBS. Like Negroes combing
Pan-Afro heads & reading Richard Wright's Native Son, as aristocratic sons & daughters engulf Old Glory in a sea of flames, like a Buddhistic monk in his moment
of martyrdom... in a vacuum of self-immolation. As Men-of-Death charges through bamboo webs of vegetation... waving arms like octopuses frantically moving their tentacles in a microsecond of euphoric madness. Like a platoon of samurais gathering in an Oriental marketplace; wielding honed swords of steel, slaughtering, killing like a raging Typhoon... like Calley's Boys machine-gunning their way through some foreign village... as black Phalluses poke through Hong Kong Charlie garments like hot rods of smouldering iron penetrating reddish wells of love... Dalian surrealism, as Algerian heads & hands are lopped off like Genghis Khan massacring Afghan peasants in a frenzy of lordly arrogance! As Dogfaces curse themselves... moan over un-mitigated bonds of servitude. Still, robotic warriors remain enthralled by a plastic record turning, spinning on a mystical turntable... as Blacks & Whites mingle under Teutonic

    lights, as Wagner's ghost loiters outside; Negroes hang, dangle, swing limply from oak trees in the Southern States... as little boys cling to widowed skirt tails, as mighty trees scream & weep all night for dead colored folks. As Whites, Reds, and Blacks sing in acidic unison; Jim Crowism shattered like Asiatic babies' brains being blown out… becoming fragments of dust dancing on Wind's carousel of pain, as Time passes in circles, as British merchants bury feudalistic heads in Lady Opium's powdery bosom… electronic beats bombard gyrating bodies… seminal souls shimmering under lights of joy, in an American **capsule of lyrics.**

THE ADDICT AND HIS DAUGHTER

Rochester, NY Summer '89

A hollow-cheeked addict
    Eyes liquefying quietly, pudgy
        Fingers squeezing a bony knee.

NOSTALGIA SOMETIMES ENCIRCLES A MAN

Nostalgia sometimes encircles a man
like the wintry wind, making him draw his coat
tightly and reside in the warmth that it provides.

UNTITLED #8

...like a Bataan soldier fornicating
with Starvation... a young troop lay
defenseless in his bed, as Lady Aids
presses her Circean-like body against him.
She slithers up and down his little frame;
brushing her bare breast against his exposed chest, ever so often...
kissing him with her pneumonic lips... suffocating
him slowly, oh so slowly.

MY HEART POUNDS LIKE THE BRITISH

My heart pounds like the British

Drummers

In preparation for war.

And I feel,

I'll be beaten to death!

If I sit here

And just watch you.

VISIONS OF LOVE

Black gal curled
Like a Persian cat upon a sofa…
Sliced by the moon's silvery blades.

AFTERTHOUGHTS
OF A TROUBLED LOVE AFFAIR

Violently/soft we came together
Like two Ninjas simultaneously
Assassinating each other,
In a battle of Oriental intrigue…,
Realizing as pleasant carnal Death
Gathered us under its illusory wings,
That Deception had taken flight on this
Joyous eve.

OPPRESSION is
when a Man denies a Child
that precious right to bloom
like a mystical Flower… longing for God's
invigorating rays of spiritual salvation.

HUMANS ARE LIKE FLOWERS

Humans are like flowers resting in the arms
of Earth; waiting passionately for
some passing bee laden with Life's pollen....

A CHILD'S SMILE IS LIKE A THOUSAND TWINKLING

A child's smile is like a thousand twinkling
stars adorning the breast of heaven.

Philosophical Roads

APATHY I

Apathy can eventually manifest itself
into a suicidal beast with cannibalistic whims,
that wishes nothing more; than to drink the toxic blood of ungodly
Beings…
whose most profound pleasures are found in
the mental <u>chalices of inactivity</u>.

THE SCORPIAN DILEMMA

Aquila struggled vehemently to remove itself
from the clutches of the tainted Polity-Snake
that crawled around within its very guts, as Eternity watched,
and shook its head in utter disgust.

THE PENDULUM OF SELF-PITY

The <u>pendulum of self-pity</u> will eventually
bring about the hypnotic state of uselessness.

OPPRESSION is
when a Nation's Supreme Court
elects to cast aside a country's
Constitutional foundation…
for Laissez Faire's Midasian caress.

IN SEARCH OF CONTRAST

Two kings of distinct pigmentations sought to build individual kingdoms of different colors and magnitude. But sad to say, their Minds would not stand
for such outlandish foolery, opting to vary only their toilet habits.

CROSSROADS

Every man must cross the thresholds of mankind's conditioned madness before he can bathe in the illusion of earthly sanity.

JUNGLE OF REASONING

Two Primates were found sitting in the Jungle of Reasoning, watching film clippings that expounded upon the basic construct of various political systems. One professed that he believed in Democracy, while his colleague favored Communism. Ironically, they both wore fur coats in the dead of Summer.

WEREWOLF II

Beware of any Nation that shows
signs of Werewolf-like tendency…
that is, a country that fears any
verbal crosses that sparkle with Truth.

BANISHMENT

I dreamt
last night
that Man
cast McCarthy
out of the Garden of Democracy.

HUMANITARIANS ARE KNOWN

Humanitarians are known
to commit hara-kiri after
numerous/intensive occasions
with Knowledge.

RUSSIAN MODERNISM

In the USSR,
Brezhnevism looked like
Genghis Khan galloping…
Trampling through Afghanistan.

So much
For Russian modernism.

DICHOTOMY OF PHRASEOLOGY

Patriotism, Collectivism, and Nationalism
stood upon their own personal islands of political
ideologies, and vehemently tossed verbal & physical objects at each other;
each proclaiming their right to exist, as the
The world watched in bewilderment;
closing their eyes
to the threesome's insane antics.

THE LITTLE MAN OF LIVING WALKED

The little Man of Living walked
Into the Valley of Life
With a Cain-like mentality; he never
Returned home to tell anyone
About it.

PARITY IN LIFESTYLES

Parity in technology
oftentimes frightens
strong Nation….

AN ICEBERG'S DEADLY BLADE

When a Nation's personal ego becomes as inflated as many believed the Titanic to be indestructible, there's a good chance, one's prospect of encountering an iceberg's deadly blade is quite likely.

THE SONG OF SIRENS

If a Man ties himself fervently to a Nation;
then he's also a suspect for suicide
when the Sirens of Nationalism call....

CANNIBALISM

When a Nation feels that it's dying, it will become quite cannibalistic...
even feeding upon itself at times, like an animal
chewing off its own leg after being
caught in a trap.

ANGST I

The fear of being alone can be like man's secularized concept of God's imminent return… that only extroverted sinners will perish in Gehenna. While the earthly Spokesmen of God's Word will flourish eternally in some cinematic kingdom in the sky.

BIRDS I

Two birds were flying through the city lanes when they spotted a Primate with a slingshot in his hand. Neither one of them exchanged a tweet as a biospheric stone struck one of them squarely in the breast. The wounded bird fell to the ground... blood squeaked from its wound. His partner, Sartre, flew away swiftly, never bothering to look back.

REAL LIVING

Once there was a man whose foot had become entangled within the stirrup of a green horse, yes, a beast that looked like a Unicorn in mind. How unfortunate for the man, though, because when he encountered a calm River that seemed as peaceful as real Living… they both drowned.

SLIMY QUICKSAND

Once upon a time, there was a little boy that walked blindly into a pit of slimy quicksand, that held him fast like a multitude of sightless followers of Moloch being repetitiously recycled... enslaved... adhering; placing their souls in the hull of a religious Ship that's filled with deadly holes, while life rafts of salvation dangle quietly in their faces. Still, they reach for nothing, while locked in the arms of Fear. Hypnotically, Moloch's servants yell out for their household Gods... whose ears resemble steel-alloys of Nature.

The little boy found himself flailing needlessly; he stopped and thought for a moment, looked up, and grabbed hold of one strong branch that dangled in front of him, and gently pulled himself free of the murderous Mud.

THE LORD IS MY SHEPHERD

The Lord is my shepherd, I shall not want, except to live and understand myself first, before I try and decode Him.

THE ROOTS OF A CHILD'S DEATH

The
roots of a child's
death lie in the core
of man's knowledge of Self…

THE ANT THAT QUIETLY TURNED AWAY....

One day an ant returned from toiling
in the Fields of Life, paused in front
of his tiny doorway. His feelers moved
vigorously like a confused human might pace
across a room in the act of fanaticism
...the Ant quietly turned away, leaving the Queen
to indulge in her ceaseless folly.

DREAM II

I dreamt last night of a mighty Panther devouring a dead, tainted Eagles flesh...which seemed so unusual. Still, I stood there watching as a powerful feline started gagging, heaving from its very guts, rancid chunks of unholy meat... as a majestic Eagle rose from a warm, disheveled carcass and sailed into God's Universe.

Peace be With You

*

Special thanks to my illustrator,
Hampton R. Olfus, Jr., who obviously
felt the same cosmic vibrations as I did;
when I presented to him the rough drafts of
the drawings that I desired for this little book.

* * * * * * * * *

ABOUT THE AUTHOR

Arthur Lee Conway is a native of Charlottesville, Virginia, and has attended the University of Maryland University College, graduating with an A.A. in Business Administration.

He is the author of WALKING THROUGH THE MIST OF LIFE, THE STRANGE WAYS OF DRAGONS, and has written his third book: THE POETIC VIBRATIONS OF A MATURED BUTTERFLY: POEMS AND PARABLES.

www.ingramcontent.com/pod-product-compliance
Lightning Source LLC
Chambersburg PA
CBHW051454290426
44109CB00016B/1754